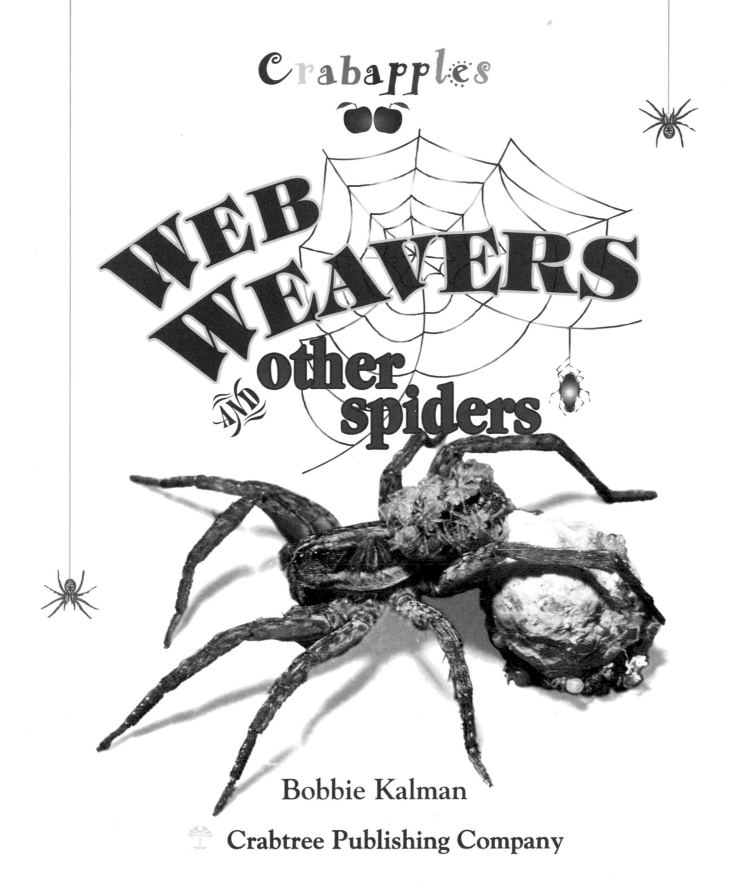

Crabapples

WEB WEAVERS and other spiders

Bobbie Kalman

Crabtree Publishing Company

Crabapples

created by Bobbie Kalman

For my sweet Osia

Editor-in-Chief
Bobbie Kalman

Writing team
Bobbie Kalman
Niki Walker
Janine Schaub

Managing editor
Lynda Hale

Editors
Petrina Gentile
Niki Walker
Greg Nickles

Computer design
Rose Campbell

Photo research
Hannelore Sotzek

Photographs
Frank S. Balthis: page 30
Michael Cardwell & Associates: pages 6, 7 (bottom)
Patrick H. Davies: page 9
Property of James Kamstra: page 31
Robert McCaw: cover, pages 4 (inset), 14, 14-15, 16 (both),
   17, 21, 26, 28
Rod Planck/Tom Stack & Associates: pages 10, 20 (top)
Photo Researchers, Inc.: Cosmaos Blank: page 19 (bottom);
   Ray Coleman: page 19 (top); Stephen Dalton: page 13;
   Martin Dohrn/SPL: page 18; Tom McHugh: pages 8, 27;
   Nuridsany and Perennou: page 11; L. West: page 29 (top)
James H. Robinson: title page, pages 4, 5 (both), 12,
   20 (bottom), 22 (both), 23, 24-25, 29 (bottom)
A. B. Sheldon: pages 7 (top), 12 (inset)

Color separations and film
Dot 'n Line Image Inc.

Printer
Worzalla Publishing Company

Crabtree Publishing Company

350 Fifth Avenue
Suite 3308
New York
N.Y. 10118

360 York Road, RR 4,
Niagara-on-the-Lake,
Ontario, Canada
L0S 1J0

73 Lime Walk
Headington
Oxford OX3 7AD
United Kingdom

Cataloging in Publication Data
Kalman, Bobbie
   Web weavers & other spiders

(Crabapples)
Includes index.

ISBN 0-86505-632-3 (library bound)   ISBN 0-86505-732-X (pbk.)
This book provides an overview of spiders, covering their
physical characteristics, web-building, mating behavior, and
defense techniques.

1. Spiders - Juvenile literature. I. Title. II. Series: Kalman,
Bobbie. Crabapples.

QL458.4.K35 1996   j595.4′4   LC 96-42408
                                                      CIP

What is in this book?

What are spiders?

Many people think spiders are insects, but they are not. Insects have six legs. Spiders have eight. A spider's body has two sections, but an insect's has three. Many insects have wings and antennae, but spiders do not.

A spider is an **arachnid**. Ticks, mites, and scorpions are also arachnids. They are relatives of spiders. Arachnids are **arthropods**, animals that have legs and joints but no backbone.

Spiders are divided into two groups— **true spiders** and **mygalomorphs**. Most spiders are true spiders. Their jaws move from side to side. Big, hairy spiders belong to the mygalomorph group. They move their jaws up and down.

There are over 34,000 known types, or **species**, of spiders. There are many more species that have not yet been found. Spiders are very important because they eat insects. Without them, there would be too many insects on earth!

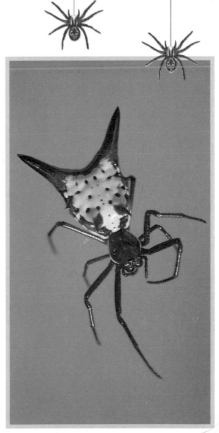

A spider's body

Spiders come in many shapes, sizes, and colors. Some are smaller than a pinhead. Others are as large as a frisbee. Some have short, wide bodies, and others are long and thin. Even though spiders may look different, their bodies have many things in common.

The spider's jaws are called **chelicerae**. They have fangs at their tips.

Inside each fang is a tube that pumps out poison, or **venom**, when a spider bites.

A spider uses its **palps** to hold prey. Males also use them during mating.

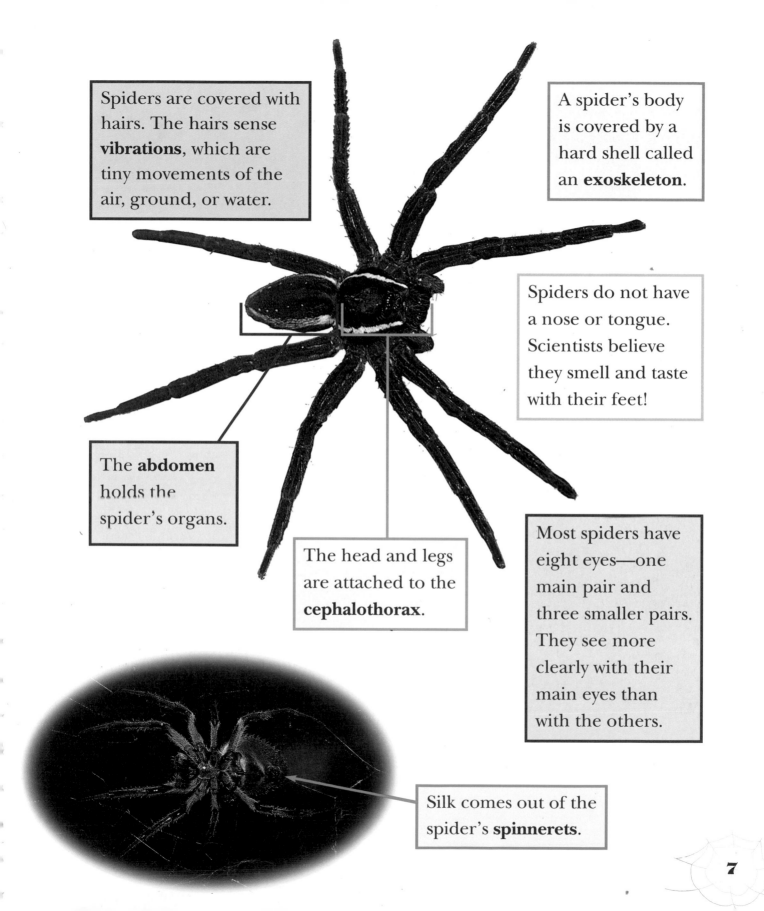

Spiders are covered with hairs. The hairs sense **vibrations**, which are tiny movements of the air, ground, or water.

A spider's body is covered by a hard shell called an **exoskeleton**.

Spiders do not have a nose or tongue. Scientists believe they smell and taste with their feet!

The **abdomen** holds the spider's organs.

The head and legs are attached to the **cephalothorax**.

Most spiders have eight eyes—one main pair and three smaller pairs. They see more clearly with their main eyes than with the others.

Silk comes out of the spider's **spinnerets**.

What do spiders eat?

Spiders are **carnivores**, or meat eaters. Most spiders eat insects or other spiders. Some larger spiders eat birds, fish, mice, lizards, snakes, or frogs.

All spiders use venom to stun or kill their prey. They pump the poison into their victim by biting it with their fangs. The venom quickly kills insects and other small prey. Larger prey, such as birds and frogs, are stunned by the poison and cannot escape.

Spiders do not chew their food—they drink it. They inject a special liquid into their prey to turn its insides to juice. They then suck up the juice and leave behind the empty shell of the body.

9

Where do spiders live?

Spiders are found in different **habitats** around the world. A habitat is the place where an animal or plant lives. Spiders live in caves, forests, fields, deserts, and swamps. Antarctica is the only place in the world where spiders have not been found.

The Eurasian water spider, shown right, is the only spider that lives, eats, and lays its eggs underwater. It attaches its cup-like web to plants that grow in the water. To breathe, the spider swims to the surface, collects air, and fills the web with air bubbles.

Silk spinners

Not all spiders build webs, but they all spin at least one kind of silk. Some make up to six kinds! They use the silk to build homes, escape from danger, protect their eggs, or trap prey.

Silk begins as a liquid inside the spider's body. It dries and hardens as it comes out of the spinnerets. The spinnerets act as tiny fingers and tug on the silk thread. The harder they pull it, the stronger it becomes.

Most spiders are like mountain climbers. They trail a line of stretchy **dragline silk** behind them. They attach the end of the dragline to a secure object such as a branch or rock.

As the spider travels, it lets out more silk. When it feels threatened, it jumps or drops away from the danger. It hangs on its dragline until the threat is gone and then climbs back up the thread.

Web weavers

About half of all spiders build webs. They are born knowing how to build them. Knowing something without being taught is called **instinct.** Spiders build webs to capture prey. Insects cannot escape from the sticky traps. Larger prey is tangled in a web and gets tired when it tries to escape. Tired prey is slow and easy to catch.

A web also protects a spider from enemies. Web weavers do not see well, but they have an excellent sense of touch. When its web is bumped or shaken, a spider scurries away and hides.

15

 # Webs

No two spider webs are exactly the same, but three basic types are **orb webs**, **sheet webs**, and **funnel webs**. An orb web, below left, is often woven between tree branches. Sheet webs, below right, often look like hammocks. Funnel webs, far right, are like sheet webs, but they have a hole near the center. The hole is joined to a tube of silk. The spider sits in this tube and waits for insects to land on the web.

Some webs are built and shared by up to a thousand spiders. **Community webs** are large enough to cover a field or tree!

Many spiders build a new web each night. Most are made in less than one hour! Webs are built with both sticky and dry silks. The spider walks on only the dry strands so that it does not get stuck on its own web.

The hunters

Spiders that do not weave webs have other ways to catch their prey. Some hide and surprise their victims with a sneak attack. Others stalk their prey.

The raft spider, shown below, sits on floating leaves or branches and dangles its legs in the water. When it feels the vibrations made by a fish, the spider dives into the water and grabs it. It then drags its prey onto land and eats it.

The net-throwing or ogre-faced spider, shown right, makes a tiny web that it holds with four of its feet. It throws this net over small insects to trap them.

The trapdoor spider, shown below, lives in a narrow tunnel in the ground. It covers the entrance with a silk sheet and dirt. The spider waits just below this door until it feels an insect moving nearby. Then it springs out and pounces on its prey.

Mating

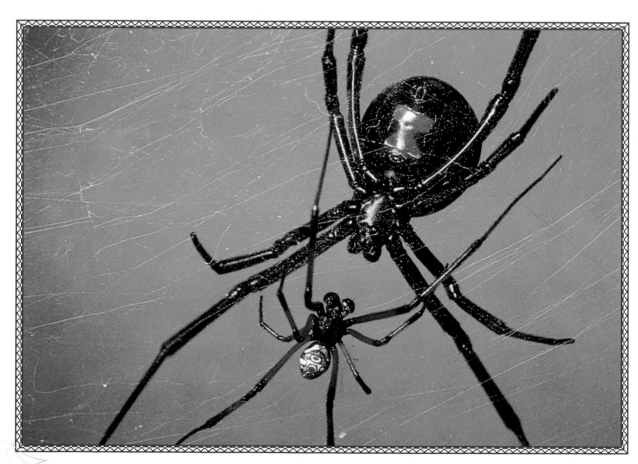

Most spiders are **solitary**, which means they spend much of their life alone. A male and female spider must mate to have babies, however.

Mating can be dangerous for males. They are smaller than females. A female, such as the one above, often mistakes a male for prey!

About a week after spiders mate, the female lays her eggs on a sheet of silk. She then wraps them in a tough sac made of many layers of silk. Some egg sacs hold only a few eggs, and others hold thousands!

To hide their eggs from hungry enemies, many spiders disguise the sacs with plants, insect bodies, or sand. Others, like the fishing spider above, carry their sac in their jaws or attached to their spinnerets.

Baby spiders
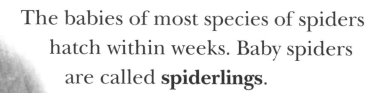

The babies of most species of spiders hatch within weeks. Baby spiders are called **spiderlings**.

Only a few types of spiders care for their babies. The wolf spider, shown left, lets her babies ride "piggyback" for up to ten days. The green lynx spider, shown below, guards her spiderlings in the nest.

Some spiderlings stay together for a few days after hatching. When they start to get hungry, though, spiderlings become a threat to one another. They must leave home quickly to avoid being eaten!

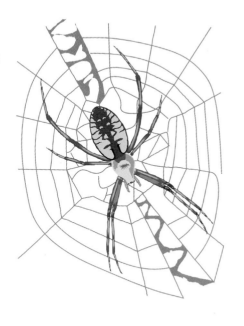

Ballooning is the fastest way to leave. A spiderling climbs to a high spot, points its spinnerets toward the sky, and shoots out a string of silk. The wind catches the silk and carries away the young spider. Some spiderlings can drift great distances on a breeze.

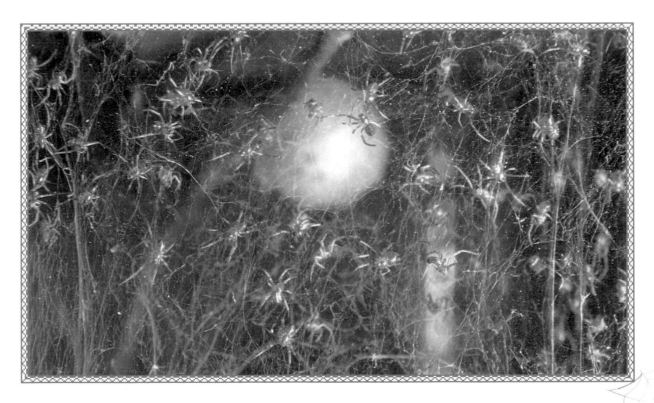

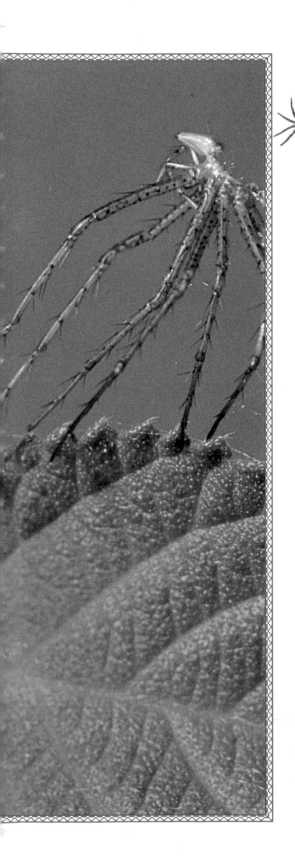

Growing up

Most young spiders grow quickly. Within a few weeks after hatching, they are fully grown. Many of these spiders live less than one year. On the other hand, some mygalomorphs live 20 to 30 years. They take four to ten years to become adults.

Young spiders grow by **molting**, or shedding, their hard exoskeleton. During a molt, the old skin cracks and the spider pulls its body out of the shell. While its new skin is soft, the spider is able to grow. In about two hours, the skin hardens into a larger exoskeleton. Some spiders continue to molt after they are adults, even though they do not grow. They simply replace their worn-out shell.

Molting is a dangerous time for spiders because they are helpless and cannot fight. Enemies often kill a spider while its body is soft and unprotected. Many spiders die when they cannot pull themselves out of their old skin.

Spider enemies

Spiders have many **predators**. Predators are animals that hunt and eat other animals. Birds, wasps, scorpions, snakes, lizards, and frogs all eat spiders.

Spiders avoid their natural enemies by running and hiding. If a spider cannot escape, it sometimes tries to scare the attacker. It raises itself on its back legs and shows its fangs.

Most spiders fight only when they are forced to defend themselves. They wrestle their attacker and try to bite it. Some spiders spit venom at their enemy. Others shoot out a stream of gluey spit.

Some mygalomorphs attack their enemies with hair! They rub their body with their back legs to scrape off special hairs that are coated with poison. The hairs make the enemy's eyes and nose itch and water. Sometimes they even blind the predator for a short time.

Spider disguises

Many spiders have colors and markings that **camouflage** them, or help them blend in with their surroundings. Camouflage helps spiders hide from enemies, and it also helps them surprise prey. Some spiders have the same coloring as bark or sand. Others, such as the crab spider below, can change color to match the flower on which they are sitting.

Some spiders **mimic**, or imitate, other creatures. The ant-mimic spider, shown right, waves its palps so they look like antennae. It also holds one pair of legs off the ground to look as though it has six legs. It wants to be mistaken for an ant because most predators know that ants are fierce fighters and they taste bad.

Others, such as the bola spider below, mimic their surroundings. When in danger, it pulls its legs around its body, making it look like a bird dropping!

People and spiders

Only a few types of spiders are able to harm humans. The black widow, the brown recluse, and the Australian funnel-web spider are the most poisonous. Their bites cause pain and illness but seldom lead to death.

In the past, a bite from one of these spiders could kill a person. Today an **antivenin** needle helps people recover quickly from bites.

On the other hand, some spiders are in danger from humans. Mygalomorphs, such as the Mexican redknee tarantula, are popular pets. Trappers have taken so many of them from the wild that they are in danger of becoming **extinct**, or disappearing. If you would like to have one of these spiders as a pet, make sure that it is **bred in captivity**. Spiders bred in captivity are not taken from the wild.

Words to know

antivenin A treatment that fights the effects of spider venom

arachnid An animal with eight legs, two body sections, and no wings or antennae

arthropod An animal that has legs and joints but no backbone

camouflage Colors or markings on an animal's body that help it blend in with its surroundings

carnivore An animal that eats only meat

exoskeleton The hard outer shell that covers a spider's body

mimic To act or appear as something else

mygalomorph The name given to a spider that is large, hairy, and moves its jaws up and down rather than from side to side

predator An animal that eats other animals

prey An animal hunted by another for food

spinneret An opening on the underside of a spider's body out of which silk comes

true spider The name given to spiders that are not mygalomorphs; their jaws move from side to side

vibration A quivering or shaking of the air, ground, or water, caused by the movements of creatures

Index

3 4 5 6 7 8 9 0   Printed in the U.S.A.   6 5 4 3 2 1 0 9